Social Security

FOR

State and Local
Government Employees

SOCIAL SECURITY

FOR

STATE AND LOCAL GOVERNMENT EMPLOYEES

A GUIDE TO SOCIAL SECURITY PROVISIONS
THAT CONCERN MANY PUBLIC EMPLOYEES AND TEACHERS~
THE GOVERNMENT PENSION OFFSET
AND THE WINDFALL ELIMINATION PROVISION

DANIEL W. RYAN, MPA, CEBS

FOREWORD BY
JAMES MCNAMEE
PRESIDENT
ILLINOIS PUBLIC PENSION FUND ASSOCIATION

WINDY CITY
PUBLISHERS

SOCIAL SECURITY FOR STATE AND LOCAL GOVERNMENT EMPLOYEES
A GUIDE TO SOCIAL SECURITY PROVISIONS THAT CONCERN MANY PUBLIC EMPLOYEES AND TEACHERS~
THE GOVERNMENT PENSION OFFSET AND THE WINDFALL ELIMINATION PROVISION

© 2020 by Daniel W. Ryan. All rights reserved.

DISCLAIMER

Windy City Publishers
2118 Plum Grove Road, #349
Rolling Meadows, IL 60008
www.windycitypublishers.com

Published in the United States of America

ISBN:
978-1-941478-89-9

Library of Congress Control Number:
2020901408

Cover Image: ImagePixel/Shutterstock.com

WINDY CITY PUBLISHERS
CHICAGO

FOR ADDIE

Contents

FOREWORD

RETIREMENT INCOME IS OFTEN DESCRIBED as a "three-legged stool" consisting of a pension, Social Security, and personal savings.

For employees of state and local government, those legs are structured and operate differently than your private sector relatives and neighbors. The pension systems fortunately are still there, not having given way to the less stable 401(k) approach. Your personal savings is likely through a public employee deferred compensation plan under Section 457 or an educator's savings plan under 403(b). These are valuable, voluntary plans which are highly utilized to the great betterment of public servants.

Your expected benefits from Social Security may or may not be the same as other working Americans. It all depends on whether or not you participate in Social Security in the classroom, fire house, police station, city hall or elsewhere in public service.

It is estimated that 28% of state and local government employees do not participate in Social Security. Many are public school teachers and those in fire/police/EMS. In some states, virtually no public employees are in Social Security. This materially affects their future retirement benefits. These public servants need to know the rules and their projected benefits in order to plan for a secure retirement.

To achieve that goal, a staff member at the Illinois Public Pension Fund Association (IPPFA) has written this book. Daniel Ryan is retired from careers as a municipal treasurer and a union-employer benefit fund administrator. He is also a long term police pension plan trustee and has worked with IPPFA since 2017, primarily on research as well as communicating benefits to active and retired police and fire professionals.

This material on Social Security first appeared in Dan's book for Illinois public safety personnel. It has been expanded and updated here with the goal of providing a complete picture of the impact of public employment on Social Security benefits nationwide. The information is presented in an easy to read, conversational manner by an author who understands the subject matter and the need for it to be understood by public servants.

There is presently proposed legislation that would materially change the *Windfall Elimination Provision*. This is discussed in the book and this matter is worth keeping an eye on by all stakeholders. The proposed changes could improve the fairness of the treatment of many public employees.

Enjoy the book, and thank you for your career commitment to serving others.

JAMES McNAMEE
President
Illinois Public Pension Fund Association (IPPFA)
Elgin, Illinois
March 2020

INTRODUCTION

THERE ARE TWO TYPES OF Public Sector professionals who are impacted by the Social Security program: those who are enrolled *in* Social Security during their government and teaching careers and those who are *not*.

There are more than six million state and local employees who do not participate in Social Security during their public service years. The information in this book is specifically directed toward those people and their families.

My interest in this subject dates back to my time as Finance Director for the Village of Skokie, Illinois. It was in the late 1980s and we were dealing with a lot of rumors and misinformation about the Social Security benefits that would be paid to our police officers and firefighters. This workforce does not participate in Social Security, setting them apart from the rest of the Village workforce in finance, public works, public health and other departments. We heard a lot of talk to the effect that the fire/police group would not receive *any* Social Security, even from credit they earned at other jobs. Another rumor said they would get one-half of what they earned; still another rumor put it at 40%. Someone told me that a retired firefighter was getting $9 a month from Social Security. Really?

The Human Resources Director and I set out to get the right story. We researched the subject, obtained the publications, and met with a Social Security "field rep" at the Evanston, Illinois office. We came away with a pretty good understanding and held a series of meetings with the employees to explain their federal benefits.

What we learned back then has been updated over the years, but the core is essentially unchanged. The key takeaways are:

> Public employees who participate in Social Security at their government job earn and receive the exact same benefits as their private sector counterparts.

> Public employees who do *not* participate in Social Security while in government or education often qualify for Social Security benefits from their private sector work before, during and after their public service careers.

> Public employees who earn pensions from work that is *not* covered by Social Security are subject to some different Social Security rules and benefit formulas than those whose career work *is* covered under Social Security. These special formulas are intended to be fair and generally do not punish or penalize public servants when compared to private sector workers with similar lifetime earnings.

> The special formulas appear complex, but their essential operation can be easily understood.

> Finally, while there is no critical need for modifying these laws, legislation which has been introduced could smooth out the potential unwarranted impact on some public employees. This legislation should be understood and followed closely by all concerned.

Information to Follow

We'll start with an explanation and a little history lesson as to why some public employees do not participate in Social Security and how that works out nationwide. Next, a basic overview of Social Security is presented, with emphasis on how employees at varying wage levels are treated. After that, we cover the two major provisions that affect public employees who work *outside* the Social Security system (and compare this to how it works for those *inside* Social Security). We'll look at the Social Security benefits of a group of hypothetical retirees, covering those inside and outside of Social Security for their main careers. The goal is to both explain the benefits and examine how fairly the Social Security rules treat everyone. This will include a discussion of some merit-based legislation that is being seriously discussed at the time of publication.

We'll conclude with a conversation on some commonly heard rumors about public employees and Social Security, a summary of all the material plus a Q&A, and then close with some resources that the reader can use to explore this subject further.

During the discussion I'll sometimes use the shorthand "SSA" to represent Social Security, as in Social Security Act—or—Social Security Administration.

DANIEL W. RYAN
Skokie, IL
March 2020
Dkryans514@yahoo.com

1 STATE AND LOCAL EMPLOYEES AND SOCIAL SECURITY

WHY ARE SOME PUBLIC EMPLOYEES OUTSIDE OF SOCIAL SECURITY?

Pretend that you could travel back to 1787 Philadelphia. You would observe thirteen guys sitting around a table at Independence Hall banging out a draft of what will become the U.S. Constitution (and they didn't have Microsoft Word to assist them). A big issue then was the relationship between the federal and state governments. Nobody wanted the federal level to be superior. This played out in some ugly ways (slavery) but also had considerable merit, both philosophically and operationally. After the debate was over, the national government was given some express and strongly implied powers, and the rest were left to the states explicitly or generally under the 10th Amendment.

This seems kind of quaint and outdated now, given that the Feds can dangle grant money in front of the states and get them to change speed limits. But this concept of federalism is still a guiding principle of our country; the national government and the states are each sovereign and draw their powers from the constitution. Affairs within a state are generally left to the state.

Does this have anything to do with the fact that Chicago firefighters or Cincinnati teachers don't pay into Social Security? Actually, yes. When the SSA was established, state and local government employees were excluded from participating due to concerns about constitutionality. The public employer-employee relationship was considered to be purely a state affair (and thus beyond the role of the national government). Also, the employer "match" of employee payroll contributions was seen as a tax on one level of government by another.

In time, constitutional concerns mostly abated and amendments to Social Security allowed the states and their local governments to participate. Specifically in 1950, under the *Section 218 Amendment to Social Security Act*, Congress allowed the states to enroll public workers in Social Security if they were not covered by a state or local retirement system. In 1954, this authority was expanded to allow state and local employees to participate even if covered by a pension plan.

Many states, but not all, chose to extend Social Security coverage to their workers. Each of the fifty states entered into agreements with the Social Security Administration that defined who would or would not be covered by Social Security. For those reading this book, your coverage or lack of coverage under Social Security as a public employee is governed by the decisions made in the past, mostly in the 1950s.

You can learn a lot about the Section 218 amendment and subsequent changes from two excellent sources. The first is the Social Security Administration website, *ssa.gov*. Look for the SLGE Home (State Local Government Employer) and also Section 218 Training, among other sub-sections. The second source is the National Conference on State Social Security Administrators (*ncsssa.org*). It turns out that each state has a designated administrator (both an entity and an actual person) who is the liaison to the federal government on issues of Social Security coverage for state and local employees. The conference website has a lot of good general information PLUS the contact information for your state's administrator.

WHAT IS THE IMPACT OF THIS HISTORY ON SOCIAL SECURITY COVERAGE TODAY?

As Jim McNamee mentioned in his Foreword, approximately 28% of state and local employees do not participate in Social Security while in public service. This includes 40% of public school teachers and over 65% of police officers and firefighters. Most public employees in Alaska, Colorado, Louisiana, Maine, Massachusetts, Nevada and Ohio are not in Social Security. This list can be expanded for public school teachers to include California, Connecticut, Georgia, Illinois, Kentucky, Missouri, Rhode Island and Texas (*i.e.*, most teachers in these states—and the District of Columbia—are excluded from Social Security).

Social Security coverage may vary greatly within the borders of some states. In California, many state and local employees enrolled in the California Public Employees Retirement System (CalPERS) are *in* Social Security. However, teachers enrolled in the statewide educators' fund (CalSTRS) are *not in* Social Security. Within a school district, supervisors and administrative employees will tend to be in Social Security; teachers will be excluded. Adeptly characterized in a *TeachersPensions.org* white-paper, "these divergences have no particular policy justification other than historical precedent." (See References).

In Illinois, most local fire and police are excluded from SSA participation, along with the state university system, public school teachers, all employees of Cook County and the City of Chicago, and some state employees. County workers other than Cook County and municipal workers other than Chicago are *in* Social Security. In the case of police and fire, small town employees were placed in Social Security. Some of those small towns eventually became big towns and established their own police or fire pension fund. But they maintained their participation in Social Security for fire and police. Other communities entered into the so-called 218 agreements to participate in Social Security for all employees. Talk about a hodgepodge.

THREE COPS WALK INTO A BAR...

After an Illinois-based regional training program, three police officers stop for a cold one to let traffic clear. One officer is from Oak Park. He is covered by an Illinois Article 3 "downstate" police pension and is not in Social Security for his police work. One cop is from Algonquin. He also has Article 3 pension coverage but is *in* Social Security. The reason is that when the deal was cut with SSA, Algonquin was a small town protected by a few officers with no local pension system. But today it's a full-blown city with a police pension fund. Because of the state/SSA deal, he and his coworkers are in Social Security forever. The third officer is from Bedford Park. She is in the Illinois Municipal Retirement Fund (IMRF) due to the small population of that community and is also in Social Security.

What's the point of this bar story? History has created circumstances where public servants responding to the same mutual aid disaster may have different pension plans or Social Security participation without any rational justification today.

WHAT'S THE IMPACT ON SOCIAL SECURITY BENEFITS?

So we have 28% or probably 6.5 million public sector employees not participating in Social Security during their main career years. But most of these people will earn a Social Security check from their nonpublic service work before, during (part-time), and after their police/fire/teaching/other careers. The monthly check that these workers will receive from Social Security will be lower than the benefits paid to me and other employees who are in the private sector or are public sector SSA participants. This is primarily because these cops, firefighters, teachers and building inspectors spend possibly thirty years of their peak earning-time outside of the Social Security system.

In addition to that key reason for lower Social Security benefits, these public workers will have their SSA benefits from their private sector jobs calculated using modified formulas that take into account their public service career. The existence of these formulas and the way they operate are surrounded by confusion, suspicion, and in some cases, anger on the part of public employees.

But it doesn't have to be that way. Be prepared to learn all you need to know about how this works. Be open minded and patient as we work through this information, and in the end, you will be your own expert on this subject.

SOCIAL SECURITY: THE BASICS 2

SOCIAL SECURITY WAS ESTABLISHED IN 1935 as part of the New Deal legislation following the Great Depression. By 2017 it was paying $945 billion in annual benefits; now the largest program in the federal budget. The system provides base-level retirement, disability, and survivor benefits to most American workers. It is sometimes referred to as a "social insurance" program, intended to keep people above the poverty level.

Social Security is funded by employee contributions from the paycheck, an employer match of the same amount, a small amount of taxation on Social Security benefits, and interest earned on U.S. Treasury investments in the Social Security trust fund. The long-term projections for funding of the system show a need for improvement either in revenue (higher taxes), a larger contribution base, benefit modifications (reductions) or some combination of the three. Private, individual accounts as a future for Social Security have been discussed but not received favorably.

In the future, even if the Social Security trust fund balance drops to zero ($0), worker and employer contributions and taxes would cover 75% of future benefits. Author's opinion: this is certainly a gap that America can manage. It's not productive for people to proclaim that *"Social Security is not going to be there for me."* It will be.

THE BASICS: ELIGIBILITY AND RETIREMENT

Who Pays for Social Security?

Workers pay 6.2% of their covered earnings for Social Security benefits and 1.45% for Medicare. Their employer matches those same payments. Wages over a certain level ($137,700 in 2020) are not taxed for Social Security but are also not included in any benefit calculation. All workers, including those not in SSA, pay the 1.45% Medicare tax if they were hired after March 21, 1986. Their employer matches the Medicare deduction. Virtually all public employees are now paying into Medicare and will get that retiree medical benefit when they turn 65.

You've seen the Social Security deduction taken out of your paycheck when you worked in SSA covered employment. It appears under the heading "FICA." You can win a bar bet (maybe) by knowing that FICA stands for *Federal Insurance Contributions Act*, the part of the Social Security enabling legislation that sanctions the payroll deduction.

How Does Someone Earn a Benefit?

You are eligible for a Social Security benefit after you earn forty "credits" in the system. A credit is earned by receiving a certain amount of Social Security covered wages in a year. In 2020, the amount is $1,410 for one credit (it was lower in the past, it will be higher in the future). Up to four credits can be earned in one year, so the requirement is sometimes called "forty quarters" as opposed to "forty credits." Using the phrase "forty quarters" is almost 100% accurate, but a school teacher on a summer break could make a little over $5,600 and earn all four credits for that year during a single calendar quarter.

Two general truths result from the forty credit requirement. First, it takes ten years of elapsed time in Social Security to earn a benefit. Second, it's not that hard to qualify for at least a small benefit. Even if you are out of SSA for thirty years in teaching, police/fire protection or other service, there is still time before, during and after that to earn a small amount of SSA-covered wages and get your forty quarters/credits. Almost everyone I know in Illinois public safety is entitled to, or will be entitled to, a Social Security benefit. You can tell if you have earned a benefit if you received a statement from Social Security telling you so. Note that after 2011, Social Security stopped sending out statements in an effort to reduce costs. However, there was enough backlash that beginning in 2015, statements are sent out at ages 25, 30, 35, 40, 45, 50, 55, and 60 and then annually.

As a supplement or an alternative for obtaining your information (a really *good* alternative), you can register for an individual account at *ssa.gov*. More on this later.

What Benefits Are Earned?

In your public employee retirement plan, we know that you get a certain portion of your wages replaced by your pension. This is referred to in the pension world as the "replacement rate." But in Social Security, the replacement rate varies by income level. The system is **progressive**—it pays a higher rate of salary replacement to a lower income worker. Here is a snapshot of benefit levels of persons who retired in 2019 at age 65.

INCOME CATEGORY	ANNUAL WAGES	ANNUAL SSA BENEFIT	REPLACEMENT RATE
Low	$ 23,308	$ 12,451	53%
Medium	$ 51,795	$ 20,538	40%
High	$ 82,872	$ 27,208	33%
Highest	$ 127,061	$ 33,134	26%

Source: National Academy of Social Insurance (NASI), 2019

This is an important chart, so let's spend a few minutes on it. We see the average lifetime wages of retirees (indexed for inflation) broken down into four quartiles, lowest to highest. We then see each group's annual Social Security benefit and the "replacement rate" (again, the percentage of their wages that is replaced by their monthly federal benefit). We note that as wages rise, Social Security benefits rise, *but not proportionately*. The replacement rate drops as income rises.

So, someone who had average earnings in the high-quartile at $82,872 per year receives a Social Security benefit of $27,208 annually. This is $14,757 more than the average worker in the lowest category receiving $12,451 per year. But the higher paid worker is receiving only 33% of his wages returned to him or her in Social Security benefits. The lower paid person's replacement rate is 53%. And someone earning still less than the lowest amount of wages shown would have an even higher replacement, maybe as high as 90%. In Social Security, the lower wage earner receives a proportionately higher benefit.

To help illuminate the progressive nature of Social Security, we can compare it to other forms of retirement income. Let's start with a comparison to a public employee retirement system. If a police retirement plan formula provides for 70% of pay after 30 years of service, that 70% is earned by all members—patrol officer, sergeant, lieutenant and chief. The patrol officer's rate is not higher because he or she earns less than a lieutenant. But Social Security *does* take income into account; the lower paid worker's benefit rate is higher.

Another comparison would be the workings of an individual savings and investment plan. Say Fred puts $2,000 into a mutual fund each year; his coworker Jacquie invests $4,000 annually in the exact same investment fund. After thirty years, Jacquie will have twice as much money as Fred. This is true no matter what happens—investment loss, investment gain, technology boom, Great Recession—whatever. If someone puts two (or three) times as much money into an exact same account for the exact same period as the next guy, he or she will always accumulate two (or three) times as much money.

But that doesn't happen in Social Security. Looking at the NASI table we see that the highest wage earners paid more than five times as much FICA tax as the lowest earners. But their benefits are not five times as high; they are less than three times the lowest payment.

To summarize:

> *Social Security pays a higher replacement rate to lower wage earners, a much higher replacement to the lowest earning workers, and a lower replacement rate to mid-level and high-income earners.*

Why is this discussion of progressivity important? For two reasons. First, Social Security and its future is in the public debate and all citizens should understand it. Second, when we get into the discussion of the modified formulas for public employees who are *not* in Social Security, the progressive nature of SSA benefits will seriously come into play.

Non-Retirement Benefits: Disability and Survivors

As noted previously, Social Security benefits include payments to disabled individuals and survivors. The formulas used to calculate these benefits are the same as for retirement benefits and result in the same progressive effect, treating low income individuals more favorably.

Disability benefits are paid to persons who can't work due to a physical or mental disability. You do not necessarily need to have worked for ten years to qualify for disability—there is a "sliding" type scale for younger workers who could not have reasonably acquired the forty credits that is needed for retirement benefits. If a worker becomes disabled relatively early in life, a shorter period to qualify for benefits is allowed.

The determination as to whether or not an applicant is disabled is made by the Disability Determination Services office in each state. Social Security publications use the word "severe" to describe the level of physical or mental impairment that must be present in order to qualify for disability benefits. This is likely a higher standard than many public retirement funds' thresholds for a disabling condition.

There is also a "recent work test" which must be passed. Essentially, you must have been in the Social Security covered workforce for about 50% of the time during a trailing period, the length of such period established based on your age. For example, a person age 31 or older must have worked in Social Security covered employment during five years out of the 10-year period preceding the onset of the disability.

Survivors benefits to widows and widowers in the amount of the benefit earned by the decedent are payable at the Full Retirement Age (age 67 for persons born in 1960 or later) or at a reduced amount beginning at age 60. These benefits are also payable at any age if the survivor takes care of a child younger than age 16 or who is disabled. But remember that if a survivor benefit is claimed, widows and widowers are not entitled to their own Social Security benefit from their *own* work records.

HOW ARE SOCIAL SECURITY BENEFITS AFFECTED BY A NON-SSA COVERED POLICE, FIRE, TEACHER OR OTHER PUBLIC PENSION?

For public employees who are not in Social Security, the benefits that they receive for their SSA covered work are affected by their time on the job at police, fire, city hall or the classroom. In the chapters that follow, I'll describe how it is different from the general American workforce and explain why.

The two provisions that we will be talking about specifically are the subjects of separate easy-to-understand SSA publications. Those provisions are:

The *Windfall Elimination Provision* (WEP)
(SSA Publication 05-10045)

The *Government Pension Offset* (GPO)
(SSA Publication 05-10007)

These publications are appended to the material in this book. If you are reading this book a few years after publication, I suggest that you go to *socialsecurity.gov* (click on "menu" then "publications"), and download and/or print updated documents for your personal files. Perhaps more easily, a Google search for these publications by name and number should take you right to the source.

3 THE WINDFALL ELIMINATION PROVISION (WEP)

SOCIAL SECURITY BENEFITS FROM *YOUR OWN WORK RECORD* IN SOCIAL SECURITY COVERED EMPLOYMENT

We begin with a discussion of the Social Security benefits you may earn from *your own* earnings record of work you performed for employers that participated in the Social Security system. This work may have been before you entered public employment, part-time work during your professional career, or work you undertook after you retired. For this chapter, I'll be concentrating on employees who are *not* in Social Security during their public service careers. When I refer to state and local government and education employees, I'll be talking about those who are *not* in Social Security at the school, police or fire department, or other public entity.

REPLACEMENT RATES, FINAL SALARY, AND SOCIAL SECURITY

You probably have a pretty good understanding of your police, fire, teacher or similar pension. Your benefit is calculated based on the salary at the end of your career, which is then multiplied by a percentage factor based on your years of work. As noted before, this percentage in the pension world is called the replacement rate, *i.e.,* the portion of your salary that is replaced by your pension. So, 75% of final pay for thirty years of service or 50% for disability reflect replacement rates of 75% or 50% respectively, multiplied by final pay.

Social Security uses the same concept with two fairly major deviations. One difference involves how the salary for the computation is determined. The second is that varying replacement rates are used on different portions of your salary. It's a bit complicated, but understandable with a little effort. And you will need to understand the details if you really want to master your knowledge of Social Security and public pensions.

Salary Used for Social Security Calculation

In public pension systems, the salary used for pension calculations might be the average of the last four years of pay, the last five years, or maybe even just the final year. In Illinois, suburban and downstate fire and police hired before 2011 have their pension calculated based on the final rate of pay (*i.e.* the last day—technically "salary attached to the rank at the time of retirement").

In contrast, Social Security uses the highest 35 years; *almost the entire working life of a person*. But, because some of those wages were earned so long ago, the Social Security formula adjusts (*i.e.* indexes) those wages for inflation up to age 60 (specifically, earnings are indexed to wage growth in the national economy). Thus, for a person who retired in 2019 who earned $10,000 back in 1985, Social Security indexes those 1985 wages forward to $29,200 when they calculate the person's average indexed earnings over his or her 35-year total.

An important truth, especially for workers who have careers outside of Social Security: calendar years with no SSA earnings count when calculating the average earnings. They go into the formula as zero dollars—$0—for the year. Consequently, if a worker had inflation adjusted earnings of $15,000 yearly for five years, then no Social Security earnings during a public service career, then $50,000 annually for ten years, his or her average indexed earnings over the highest 35 years would be as follows:

10 years at $50,000	$500,000
5 years at $15,000	$75,000
20 years at $0	$0
Total—Highest 35 Years	$575,000
Average Annual over 35 Years	$16,430
Indexed Monthly Average over 35 Years	$ 1,369

Replacement Rates

After the average salary is calculated (called "average indexed monthly earnings" or AIME), the Social Security system then uses different replacement rates for up to three separate brackets of an individual retiree's inflation-indexed income. For persons attaining age 62 in 2020, those income brackets and replacement rates are:

First $960 in monthly earnings	**90%**
Next $4,825 in monthly earnings	32%
Over $5,785 to taxable maximum	15%

Let's look at an example of how these rates work for three different Social Security recipients:

MONTHLY AVERAGE WAGE	CALCULATION	BENEFIT	REPLACEMENT RATE
Retiree #1—$800	$800 @ 90%	$720	90%
Retiree #2—$1,500	$960 @ 90%	$1,037	69%
	$540 @ 32%		
Retiree #3—$6,900	$960 @ 90%	$2,575	37%
	$4,825 @ 32%		
	$1,115 @ 15%		

Remember the time I spent discussing the progressive nature of Social Security benefits (lower income earnings receive a higher percentage replacement). The structure and examples above show you how this comes to be. The very low paid worker ($800 monthly or $9,600 a year) gets 90% of average wages in Social Security benefit. The highest paid worker shown gets some of his or her wages replaced at 90%, most at 32%, and a portion at 15%. The highest wage earner's final replacement rate is 37%. That 37% doesn't appear anywhere in the published formulas—it's a weighted compilation of the three different published rates of 90, 32, and 15 percent.

Picture a bus of senior citizens heading out of Chicago to an Indiana casino. Virtually no two people on the bus will be receiving the same replacement rate from Social Security unless they happened to earn the exact same earnings over their lives.

Note that the formulas shown above calculate the benefit that is payable at the Full Retirement Age (FRA). That age is 66 for persons born between 1943 and 1954 and is 67 for persons born in 1960 or later. If you were born between 1955 and 1959, your Full Retirement Age is between 66 and 67. A person can retire before the FRA, as early as age 62, but with a reduction in their Social Security check and a limitation on how much they may earn in wages each year. A person can also retire later than the FRA, up to age 70, and experience an increase in monthly benefits over the amount calculated using the formula. **Your status as a public sector employee or retiree does not change any of these ages or rules.** Accordingly, you can depend on the many articles and presentations available on "claiming strategies" that explain options for drawing Social Security at various ages from 62 to 70. Your status as a government retiree does not affect any of the claiming rules.

THE WINDFALL ELIMINATION PROVISION (WEP)— A MAJOR PROVISION AFFECTING STATE/LOCAL EMPLOYEES

For public employees who are *not* in Social Security at the fire or police department or classroom or elsewhere, there is a different Social Security formula than the one described above. I'll explain it first, examine why this formula is used, and then review the fairness of this approach.

Under the *Windfall Elimination Provision*, adopted in 1983, workers who receive a pension from work outside of the Social Security system have a different benefit formula. Under this modified formula, the first increment of salary (before a so-called "bend point" in the formula) is replaced at a lower percentage than in the standard, progressive formula. Specifically, the first increment is replaced at 40%, not 90%. For persons attaining age 62 in 2020, this is how the WEP works:

First $960 in monthly earnings	**40%**
Next $4,825 in monthly earnings	32%
Over $5,785 to taxable maximum	15%

The first $960 is replaced at 40% for these workers who have a pension from work outside of Social Security, not 90%. All wage thresholds and other replacement rates are unchanged. Here's how the formula treats two hypothetical state or local agency retirees:

MONTHLY AVERAGE WAGE	CALCULATION	BENEFIT	REPLACEMENT RATE
Retiree #1—$800	$800 @ 40%	$320	40%
Retiree #2—$1,500	$960 @ 40%	$557	37%
	$540 @ 32%		

SIMPLE RULE—ALMOST

There is no simple rephrasing that captures the *Windfall Elimination Provision* (as there is for the *Government Pension Offset* to follow). But it's not overly complicated. We see that the first increment of the formula is different, reducing the amount paid by up to $480 per month. This is because the difference between 90% of the first $960, and 40% of $960, is always $480. If a particular police or fire or teaching retiree had a very small Social Security earnings record, say $500 per month in adjusted lifetime earnings, the difference would be $250.

The reduction under the WEP from the standard progressive formula varies with income. So a simple rule is pretty tough to come by. You could say that the WEP produces a Social Security benefit in 2020 that is approximately 40% to 56% lower than the standard progressive formula but never more than $480 lower. Since there is no simple formula, we follow with a method to pin it down fairly exactly.

GET IT RIGHT—SIGN UP AT SSA.GOV

A superior approach for estimating your benefit is to go to the *ssa.gov* website and register for an individual account. I have done this and it's pretty slick. I think the online security is good, but in today's world of hackers everyone should make his or her own decision. The system will ask you questions that only you know the answer to and you will realize that only SSA or the IRS would know enough to ask the questions. Once you have registered, you can examine your own record and use the data to run projections based on your status as a nonparticipating government employee outside of Social Security. This is done with the "Online Calculator (WEP Version)." Input your Social Security earnings from your *ssa.gov* account into the calculator and receive a pretty good estimate of your future benefits.

If you don't want to go so far as to open an account, you can also access the same "Online Calculator (WEP Version)" at *socialsecurity.gov*, plug in your personal earnings information from your Social Security Statement, and get an estimate.

THINGS THAT LESSEN THE IMPACT OF THE WEP

To help ensure that application of the WEP is not unfair, the law provides a few generally well-thought-out provisions to lessen its impact.

Substantial earnings. If a person has thirty or more years of "substantial earnings" in Social Security, the WEP formula does not apply even if he or she qualifies for a pension from work outside of Social Security.

Between twenty-one and twenty-nine years of SSA substantial earnings, the impact of the modified WEP formula is lessened proportionally. For example, if you have twenty-five years of substantial earnings, the first salary increment is replaced at 65% (not 40% or 90%, but 65%).

What is a year of substantial earnings? For 2019, if you made $24,675 or more, it was considered to be substantial Social Security earnings for this purpose. This amount is inflation-adjusted; it was lower in the past and will be higher in the future. Each year's requirement is spelled out in the publication 05-10045, which appears in an Appendix to this book.

Why is there this modification to the WEP? It's because people who work at an almost full-time second job, even while they are in fire, police, teaching or similar work, will have most of their SSA wages replaced in the standard formula at 32% or 15%. There is no "windfall" created if they get the first small increment at the poor man's 90%. The standard Social Security benefit formula, *not the WEP*, applies to them.

WEP does not apply to Survivor Benefits. Another concession given is that the *Windfall Elimination Provision* doesn't apply to Social Security Survivor's Benefits. So if you earned a Social Security benefit under the WEP of $557 and die before your spouse, he or she would be eligible for survivor's benefits of $1,037 (the amount of your benefit calculated using the standard non-WEP formula.)

WEP reduction is limited. Finally, the reduction under the WEP cannot be more than ½ of your public pension. This is a protection that is rarely invoked, but may help persons who have relatively low public service pensions. For this reduction, it is worthwhile to mention that if you have a pension that is from work both inside and outside of Social Security coverage, your Social Security payment can only be reduced under the WEP by no more than ½ of your *non*-Social Security covered pension.

SLIGHTLY BAD NEWS—
YOUR SOCIAL SECURITY STATEMENT *DOES NOT* REFLECT
THE IMPACT OF YOUR GOVERNMENT PENSION

This is important. The Social Security Statement that is mailed to you at certain ages or upon request does not reflect any possible changes in Social Security benefit due to your government pension from outside of SSA. This is because at the time that estimates are made, Social Security knows only so much about your pension history. Accordingly, they issue the statements without any calculation changes but with the following notices, appearing on page two of the statement:

> **Windfall Elimination Provision (WEP)**—If you receive a pension from employment in which you did not pay Social Security taxes and you also qualify for your own Social Security retirement or disability benefit, your Social Security benefit may be reduced but not eliminated, by WEP. The amount of the reduction, if any, depends on your earnings and number of years in jobs in which you paid Social Security taxes, and the year you are age 62 or become disabled. For more information, see *Windfall Elimination Provision* (Publication No. 05-10045) at www.socialsecurity.gov/WEP.

> **Government Pension Offset (GPO)**—If you receive a pension based on federal, state or local government work in which you did not pay Social Security taxes and you qualify, now or in the future, for Social Security benefits as a current or former spouse, widow or widower, you are likely to be affected by the GPO. If GPO applies, your Social Security benefit will be reduced by an amount equal to two-thirds of your government pension, and

could be reduced to zero. Even if your benefit is reduced to zero, you will be eligible for Medicare at age 65 on your spouse's record. To learn more, please see *Government Pension Offset* (Publication 05-10007) at www.socialsecurity.gov/GPO.

IS THE WINDFALL ELIMINATION PROVISION FAIR? FOUR RETIREES WALK INTO A BAR

The tavern that these four retirees walk into is across the street from a Social Security office where each has just been told what his or her SSA benefit is going to be. They have a few drinks and then start comparing notes. Here's each person's story:

> **ANDREA** has had a tough life, financially and otherwise. She's worked a lot of low paying and/or part-time jobs like waitress and hotel housekeeper. She's divorced after being married twice, never long enough (ten years) to earn a Social Security benefit from her ex-husbands' records. Her average indexed earnings over her working life are $18,000 annually. Her monthly Social Security benefit estimate at the Full Retirement Age is $1,037; which reflects a replacement rate of 69% of her SSA earnings of $1,500 per month.

> **NEIL AND KATHY** are twins. Neil was a police officer in New York who has a police department pension and was covered under SSA for his work in law enforcement. Kathy was a human resources manager for a large oil company. They each have the exact same earnings record in Social Security: average index earnings of $82,800, or

$6,900 monthly. Not surprisingly, they have the exact same Social Security benefit—$2,575 monthly or 37% of wages replaced. Neil's Social Security benefit is not affected by his government employment since both he and the city paid FICA tax on his police wages.

MICHAEL is a retired Chicago firefighter. His salary was similar to the New York police and private company salaries earned by Neil and Kathy, but Michael's career wages were earned outside of Social Security. He had some Social Security earnings however from work before taking the oath, a little self-employed construction during the fire job, and then going to work full-time for ten years after the fire department. Because he had many years of low earnings or no earnings years in his 35-year Social Security computation period, his average monthly indexed earnings are only $1,500 monthly. He properly tells the SSA office that he has a fire pension from outside of Social Security, and they give him his benefit estimate: $557 per month or a 37% replacement rate.

Like I said, the four retirees compare notes. Andrea is very pleased that her $1,037 benefit will replace so much of her low wages. Twins Neil and Kathy are at first concerned that Andrea is getting a 69% salary replacement while they are only getting 37%. Then they remember the nice lady at the SSA office describing the progressive nature of Social Security benefits. They appreciate why Andrea gets a higher replacement rate. They are satisfied with the fact that they each get over $1,500 more each month than the lower paid worker even if the replacement rate of their salaries is lower.

Neil and Kathy also observe that even though their paths to Social Security were different, they were each in the SSA system for all of their working years and are treated exactly the same for calculation of their benefits. It doesn't matter that Neil has a New York police pension and Kathy has a 401(k) plan from her private sector job. Each was in Social Security for that work and the system treats each of them *exactly* the same.

Then there's Chicago firefighter, Michael. Michael has a decision to make as to what his attitude will be towards Social Security. He has the same inflation adjusted SSA wages as Andrea—$18,000 per year—but he gets a different Social Security benefit, $557 to her $1,037. And yet he has virtually the same total career wages and Social Security replacement rate of 37% as Neil and Kathy. **Is Michael getting cheated because he has a fire pension, or is he being treated the same as everyone else with similar lifetime earnings?**

Michael and you can judge for yourselves. Following is what some people who have studied the subject have to say:

THE WINDFALL ELIMINATION PROVISION—SOME OPINIONS:

From "Turning 65, thinking about working," Stewart, JK, *Chicago Tribune*, January 30, 2011:

> Social Security uses a progressive formula to calculate benefits. Workers with relatively low lifetime earnings will have a higher wage-replacement rate than highly paid workers, meaning their monthly government benefits will account for a higher percentage of their former salaries. Without the windfall elimination provision, private sector workers who appeared to earn low lifetime wages but then also worked in government jobs not

covered by Social Security would qualify for those higher wage-replacement rates. The windfall provision aims to bring the calculation more in line with replacement rates that correspond to others with similar total earnings.

From Allison Shelton's WEP and GPO papers for the Congressional Research Service (as summarized in Alicia Munnell's book *State and Local Pensions: What Now*). This summary statement covers the *Windfall Elimination Provision* and additionally comments on the *Government Pension Offset* (see next chapter):

> Since a worker's monthly earnings for purposes of benefit calculation are averaged over a typical working lifetime rather than over the years actually spent in covered employment, a high earner with a short period of time in covered employment cannot be distinguished from an individual who worked a lifetime in covered employment at an exceptionally low wage. Thus a worker who was entitled to a state and local pension (from outside SSA) and to Social Security could qualify for the subsidized benefits associated with the progressive benefit formula. Similarly, a spouse who had a full career in uncovered employment—and worked in covered employment for only a short time or not at all—would be eligible for the spouse's and survivor's benefits. The WEP instituted a modified benefit formula for people who qualify for Social Security based on a brief work history and who have earned a pension in noncovered employment. The GPO reduces spouse's benefits for those who have a government pension in noncovered employment. Although these provisions may not produce perfect adjustments

for each individual, in the aggregate they have substantially solved the problem.

From *TeacherPensions.org*, posted on April 21, 2014 by Andrew Rotherham:

> The Social Security Windfall Elimination Provision or WEP exists to remove the windfall that the Social Security benefit formula provides to individuals who have substantial pensions from employment not covered by Social Security. Essentially, the Social Security benefit formula provides workers who spent their lives in low-paying jobs relatively higher wage replacement rates than it does for higher-paid workers. As a result, without the WEP, a worker who spent a substantial part of their career in employment not covered by Social Security would be treated as a low-lifetime earner for Social Security benefit purposes and receive the advantage of the weighted benefit formula.

From *Social Security: The Windfall Elimination Provision*, October 22, 2019 report of the Congressional Research Service:

> The *windfall elimination provision* (WEP) is a modified benefit formula designed to remove the unintended advantage, or "windfall," of the regular benefit formula for certain retired or disabled workers who spent less than full careers in covered employment and who are also entitled to pension benefits based on earnings from jobs not covered by Social Security. The reduction in initial benefits caused by the WEP is designed to place

affected workers in approximately the same position they would have been in had all their earnings been covered by Social Security.

The analyses from these four writers noted above say it better than I can. The WEP formula is not a punitive apparatus that unfairly reduces a teacher or other public servant's Social Security benefit. The WEP formula is intended to equalize replacement rates among public and private workers who have the same total lifetime wages.

There are certainly other writers who arrive at the opposite conclusion: suggesting that the WEP takes away hard-earned benefits from beleaguered public workers. None of these writers ever demonstrate that they appreciate the nature of the Social Security progressive formula. They don't acknowledge that some provisions may be needed to deal with the eventuality that a middle-income or above wage earner would earn a "windfall" by being treated like a lower income individual.

THE WINDFALL ELIMINATION PROVISION— SOME FAIRNESS CONSIDERATIONS AND LEGISLATIVE PROPOSALS

My analysis and the more scholarly reviewers endorse the general concept that the WEP is fair. However, the *Windfall Elimination Provision* is not perfect. The formula is inexact. Historical review shows that the first bend-point adjustment to 40% was a compromise between 61% favored by the U.S. House and 32% favored by the U.S. Senate. Was this compromise a good way to address the problem?

The wage and benefit examples I chose for my "walking into a bar" retiree group resulted in the exact same replacement rate for the higher earners. In practice, the WEP can over-adjust benefits to avoid a windfall or under-adjust benefits to avoid a windfall. There is evidence that, more times than not, the WEP *over-adjusts* benefits, resulting in a small loss for the retired teacher, firefighter, cop or similarly affected worker.

Legislation has been routinely introduced over the years to eliminate the WEP. But these bills that call for complete elimination never advance. They are expensive and seek to right a wrong that doesn't fully exist.

But legislation to smooth out the inexactness and probable detrimental outcome of the WEP for many retirees is now being seriously discussed. This is because, as of today, the federal government has thirty-five (35) years of earnings data on *all* Americans, regardless of whether the earnings were covered or not covered by Social Security. This information is available because the data has been captured to support the participation of all workers in Medicare beginning in 1986. Such data was not available back in the early 1980s when Congress addressed the windfall issue by compromising on a modified formula.

Serious legislation now focusses on a "proportional formula" under which the replacement rate is calculated on total wages—wages earned both inside and outside the Social Security system. Whatever rate is established using the standard 90% – 32% – 15% factors is then applied to the Social Security earnings of any retiree. Initially introduced as the *Public Service Fairness Formula* in 2015, this bill was reintroduced in 2019 as HR 3934, the *Equal Treatment of Public Servants Act of 2019*. An analysis by Social Security's actuaries found that 69% of persons affected by the WEP would see an increase of about $74 monthly. However, the balance of the group (31%) would see a reduction in the range of $55 monthly. Note that the currently proposed legislation has a "phase in" type feature wherein retirees would get the benefit of the new calculation or the current WEP approach, whichever produces a higher benefit. This would run through 2061.

Surprisingly, the bill may be cost-neutral or even provide for a small actuarial gain to the Social Security system. This is because there are some people who work a few years outside of Social Security but who don't earn a pension and are never subject to the WEP. Under the proportional formula, they would have a small reduction in their benefit when their non-Social Security covered earnings are used to set the replacement rate. This has caused some concern.

Will this legislation be adopted? I can never predict these things. There are a lot of people affected, over 6 million, but this is only 4% or so of the total covered population. Keep your eye on the news.

How to Plan

Again, if you are subject to the WEP provision, the best way to obtain a solid benefit estimate is to (a) register for an account at *ssa.gov* and then (b) use the Social Security Online Benefit Calculator WEP Version. Answer the questions and input your historical earnings information from your Social Security Statement or obtained from your account at *ssa.gov.*

Closing

The *Windfall Elimination Provision* (WEP) is the rule that most impacts the state/local government retiree who did not participate in Social Security during a public service career. It is designed to protect against that person receiving too high of a replacement rate in his or her benefit calculation; a replacement rate that is otherwise intended for low income individuals. It does not apply to persons who have substantial wages earned outside of public employment and does not apply to survivor's benefits. Overall, it is fair but imperfect and may have a slightly negative impact on many public workers. Legislation that would correct this and could reasonably be adopted has been introduced.

THE GOVERNMENT PENSION OFFSET (GPO) 4

SOCIAL SECURITY BENEFITS FROM YOUR SPOUSE'S RECORD

Let's continue, moving to the subject of benefits from a spouse's record and the related *Government Pension Offset* (GPO), adopted in 1977. Overall, this is an easier topic to master than the *Windfall Elimination Provision* (WEP). Note the GPO and the WEP are often confused for one another. They are not related.

The scope of the *Government Pension Offset* is limited; it affects only the Social Security benefits that you might receive from your wife or husband's Social Security wages. This key fact cannot not be under emphasized:

> *The Government Pension Offset only impacts the Social Security benefits that state and local government/ education employees will receive off of their spouses' records, not their own records in Social Security covered employment.*

SPOUSAL BENEFITS EXPLAINED

For the Social Security covered population, a retiree receives Social Security benefits equal to (a) the benefits earned from his or her own work record or (b) one-half of a spouse's Social Security benefit, which-ever is higher. Two examples follow:

Mark's SSA Benefit	$2,000
Sue's SSA Benefit from her own record	$800

Sue will receive the following:	
From her own record	$800
From Mark's Record	$200
Sue's Total Benefit	**$1,000**

Sue is entitled to her own SSA benefit plus a spousal benefit (sometimes called a "spousal top-off") so that her total Social Security payment is one-half of Mark's. Together, the couple will receive $3,000 (Sue's share does not come out of Mark's benefit).

A second example:

Ward's Benefit	$2,200
June's SSA Benefit from her own record	$0

June will receive the following:	
From her own record	$0
From Ward's Record	$1,100
June's Total Benefit	**$1,100**

June was at home taking care of her two sons (Wally and Theodore) and never worked enough time in SSA-covered employment to accumulate

forty credits, so she has no benefit on her own record. But she is still entitled to a spousal benefit from Ward's record of wage earnings. Together
the couple will receive $3,300.

THE GOVERNMENT PENSION OFFSET (GPO)

The *Government Pension Offset*, however, provides for a reduction in
Social Security benefits <u>from a spouse's record</u> of 66-cents for every
dollar a public employee receives from a state or municipal pension if
he or she was *not* in Social Security at their government job. An example
really isn't needed, because this can all be rephrased in a simple rule that
I'll address shortly. But since I used examples to explain how spouse
benefits work, let's look at an example of the impact of the GPO using
the same approach.

> **Bruce is an Atlanta public school teacher. His wife,
> Ellen, is a partner in a big CPA firm and she paid the
> maximum FICA tax for her career of more than forty
> years. Ellen is entitled to the highest benefit avail-
> able at Social Security's Full Retirement Age. Today
> that highest benefit is about $3,000 monthly (it can be
> higher if the retiree defers benefits until age 70).**

Let's do a quick refresher in the form of a quiz question: If the highest
Social Security benefit in the land is $3,000, what is the highest spousal
benefit available? Answer: $1,500.

So, the highest potential SSA spousal benefit for Bruce is $1,500.
However, he has a $4,000 monthly teacher pension, which will reduce
his Social Security *from Ellen's record* by 66-cents for every dollar of
teacher pension. Here's where it gets simple: a 66-cent reduction for
every dollar of a $2,250 or higher public pension from outside of Social

Security reduces *any* SSA spousal benefit to zero dollars. Let's lay it out in the same table as the other examples:

Ellen's Benefit	$3,000
Bruce's SSA Benefit from his own record	$650
Bruce will receive the following:	
From his own record	$650
From Ellen's record	<u>$850</u>
Sub-Total	$1,500
Less Offset*	<u>($850)</u>
Bruce's Total	**$650**

(*) Of course, Bruce's spousal benefit of $850 is not offset by 66-cents of *every* dollar of his $4,000 teacher pension since that would result in an offset of $2,664, far more than his or anyone's spousal benefit. Bruce simply receives no SSA spouse benefit ($0) from Ellen's earnings record because of his teacher pension and the impact of the *Government Pension Offset*.

SIMPLE RULE

Do you plan on getting a government pension of at least $2,250 or more per month? I'll bet you do. As a result of your pension from work outside of SSA, any Social Security *spousal* benefit for you will be eliminated. So, let's rephrase the whole 66-cent/dollar offset formula as follows:

Except in rare cases, a person with a pension from work outside of Social Security coverage will not receive a Social Security monthly spousal benefit from a husband or wife's record.

How's that for simplicity? You won't get a monthly benefit off of your spouse's record. Why doesn't Social Security just say that instead of taking us through the whole offset calculation? It's because there are some people who have very small public pensions—only a few hundred dollars a month—from part-time work over a short career. A substitute school teacher might be an example. Offsetting these people's entire spousal benefit is not SSA's intention, so a formula is used to minimize the impact of these low value pensions (see the discussion on fairness that follows).

Can your spouse get a Social Security benefit off of *your* SSA record? Absolutely. The GPO doesn't affect the benefits that anyone else other than you will receive.

> *The Government Pension Offset applies only to benefits that <u>you</u> receive from your <u>spouse's</u> record.*

MEDICARE FROM A SPOUSE'S RECORD

Although this book does not cover the subject of health insurance in retirement, there is an important point worth mentioning here. Access to Medicare benefits requires the same "forty credits" of employment in Medicare covered employment. Almost all workers in the country will qualify for Medicare because either (a) they work in Social Security covered employment and attain 40 credits, (b) they are in non-Social Security covered employment but their first day was on or after March 21, 1986, and they and their employer have been paying Medicare taxes, or (c) they were married for 10 or more years to someone who is Medicare eligible. If category (c) is the only way you can qualify for Medicare, the good news is that the *Government Pension Offset* does not eliminate your Medicare eligibility through a spouse's record.

DOES THE GOVERNMENT PENSION OFFSET AFFECT *SURVIVORS* BENEFITS FROM A SPOUSE'S RECORD?

Unfortunately, yes. The GPO affects both retirement *and* survivor benefits from a spouse's record. So if a person in noncovered employment is married to a person with a sizable Social Security benefit, the offset will also apply to the potential survivor benefit if the spouse in Social Security dies first. Since that benefit might be sizable, the GPO may not offset all of the benefit. It would take a public pension of approximately $4,500 to offset the highest survivor benefit under Social Security. But the offset will still be substantial and receipt of Social Security benefits as a survivor should not be depended on by a person who has a career outside of Social Security.

GPO EXCEPTION—THE LAST 60-MONTH RULE

There is a special rule that shuts off the *Government Pension Offset*, but it is rarely applicable. Under the so-called "Last 60-month Rule," if you are employed in a position for the last 60 months of employment where you both (a) contribute to Social Security and (b) are covered under the same pension plan as your previous job where you did *not* participate in Social Security, the GPO will not apply to your spousal benefit. This can occur if you work under a statewide pension plan that covers people who both participate and don't participate in Social Security, depending upon the employer's arrangement with the federal agency.

For someone working in public school teaching in Illinois, the 60-month Rule would never apply—none of our school districts participate in

Social Security for certified teachers. But in Texas and some other states, a teacher might have a career at a district that *doesn't* participate in Social Security but then spend her last 60-months (or longer) at a school district that *does* participate in Social Security.

If it is possible for you to take advantage of the 60-month Rule, be sure that you do not work in any non-SSA covered employment during those last 60 months. Don't coach or take a small part-time job anyplace that doesn't participate in Social Security. Those last 60 months must be purely in Social Security covered employment under the same pension plan where you worked outside of Social Security.

GPO PARTIAL EXCEPTION—PENSION BASED ON WORK BOTH INSIDE AND OUTSIDE SOCIAL SECURITY

In circumstances similar to the above, if a retiree has a government pension that is partially from work *in* Social Security and partially from work *outside* of Social Security, the GPO impact is prorated. For example, if Addison has a $2,000 government pension of which ½ was earned at an employer where she paid Social Security taxes and ½ was earned at a non-participating employer, then $1,000 in pension would be used in the offset formula, not the full $2,000. If this applies to you, you will need to be ready with the necessary documentation, such as a letter from the pension fund showing the ratio of participating and non-participating work.

IS THE GPO FAIR?

The *Government Pension Offset* is the law of the land so it's really not my role to convince any reader that it is a fair provision. According to the SSA publication 05-10007, the spousal benefit was created to compensate people who raised a family or were otherwise financially dependent on the spouse. Congress did not want full-time government employees who did not pay Social Security taxes to be treated in the same manner as a stay-at-home spouse or other low income American. For this reason, the *Government Pension Offset* was established in the mid-1970s.

I think that's a pretty good explanation and justification.

Also, think about the police officers in my "three cops walk into a bar" story whose police work is *in* Social Security? Two things. First, the GPO does not concern them. They do not have a pension from outside the SSA system; their police or IMRF pensions are from *inside* the Social Security system. So, the *Government Pension Offset* does not apply to them.

But if it did, would they care? The answer is no.

Look at the practical numbers. Say each officer's Social Security benefit is going to be at least $2,100 per month. For them to get a benefit from a spouse's record, their wife or husband's SSA benefit would have to be over $4,200. But that's not possible—$4,200 is well above the highest benefit payable in the country now.

So, no spousal benefit is ever paid to *anyone* who earns an average or above Social Security benefit on his or her own record. In fact, very few spousal benefits are paid at all these days now that most households are two-income.

Some summary observations:

> The cop, firefighter, teacher or similar worker who has a pension from a career outside of Social Security is not going to get an SSA retirement benefit from a spouse's record because of the *Government Pension Offset*. A survivor benefit is unlikely.

> The cop, firefighter, teacher or similar worker who is *in* SSA is technically eligible for a spousal benefit, but will

not receive one because his or her own benefit is too high to qualify for a spousal benefit. The author of this book is *not* going to get a benefit off of a spouse's record for this reason.

No part of the GPO affects the benefit that a spouse can receive from a firefighter, police officer or teacher or similar worker's Social Security record.

With the help of the Social Security Administration's own guidance, I'm ready to sign off on the belief that the *Government Pension Offset* is fair; the spousal benefit is only for non-working or low income spouses.

I'm still a little bothered with the actuality that no survivor benefit is likely to be paid to a nonparticipating worker. Perhaps the offset in sometimes-dire circumstances should be lessened for a surviving spouse with young children, maybe a 50-cent reduction for each $1 of public pension as opposed to 66-cents. But no approach like this is ever discussed when "reform" legislation is introduced. Such legislation always calls for the 100% elimination of the *Government Pension Offset*. That is not going to happen.

How to Plan

Do not plan on receiving a Social Security spousal benefit from your husband or wife's work record. The only Social Security retirement benefit will come from your own work record.

It is possible that you will receive a survivor benefit should your spouse pre-decease you, but it is unlikely. To firm that up, divide the estimated survivor benefit from our spouse's record (it appears on her/his statement from Social Security) by 0.667. If your public pension is estimated at more than the product of that division, your potential survivor benefit from Social Security is zero dollars. If your pension is less than that amount, a small federal survivor benefit will be payable.

MOST IMPORTANTLY: DON'T WORRY

As I have mentioned, there are very few spousal benefits paid in the country today under any circumstances. Don't spend a lot of time worrying about the big bad *Government Pension Offset* that only limits or eliminates your potential spousal benefit. It just makes you the same as most other people walking down the street on any given day.

And don't confuse the GPO with any other Social Security provision and avoid the use of the word "offset" in this context unless you are specifically talking about the GPO impact on spousal benefits. The word "offset" does not apply to any other applicable consideration.

Rumors 5

FALSE INFORMATION IS PROVEN TO spread faster than the truth. And there are a lot of rumors that arise out of misunderstanding of the *Government Pension Offset* (GPO) and the *Windfall Elimination Provision* (WEP). These rumors mix up the GPO and the WEP (this happens a lot), announce that some workers won't get any Social Security, declare that all public servants are impacted by special rules (even those who paid FICA taxes while working their entire lives) and state that a widow's Social Security benefits are reduced if they receive a survivor benefit from a public pension plan. And more.

We'll review some of the stories that I've heard, which will serve two purposes. First, we'll kill or validate the rumors. Second, going through this exercise will serve as a review of the subject and a means of increasing your knowledge of this topic.

> **Rumor #1: Teachers get no Social Security benefits, even if they earned the necessary credits from non-teaching work.** Patently false. The *Windfall Elimination Provision* presents a modified formula for public servants who have pensions from work outside of the Social Security system. But none of the factors in the formula are 0%. So of course, a benefit will be paid, it will just be modified to prevent the windfall.

43

Want more proof that this rumor is false? I know retired Illinois teachers who are receiving Social Security benefits. Very small benefits (they were outside the SSA system for thirty years), but they are receiving Social Security nonetheless.

> **Rumor #2: My Social Security will be offset by two-thirds of my police pension**. Mostly false. The two-thirds reduction in Social Security benefits occurs under the *Government Pension Offset* to the Social Security benefit that this police officer might receive from a <u>husband or wife's Social Security record</u>, not the officer's own earned benefits under SSA.

> **Rumor(s) #3: Chicago and suburban firefighters "pleasantly surprised" by the amount of their Social Security benefits.** This is true many times. I have friends who are retirees of both systems who were expecting to get little or no Social Security benefit because of the *Windfall Elimination Provision*. But they are receiving $500 or $650 and are quite pleased. And this benefit level is attained without any career wages that qualify as substantial earnings under Social Security.

> **Rumor #4: Participants in the Illinois Municipal Retirement Fund (and similar funds nationwide) get reduced benefits even though they contribute to Social Security on all of their wages.** Absolutely false. A public employee who works in a job that participates in Social Security is unaffected by any provisions that apply to those who work outside the system. This rumor came to me in reference to a clerical employee at a local Illinois school. The clerical staff participates in the IMRF, not the

teacher's system. This woman, who is anticipating a fairly low Social Security benefit based on her printed statement, called Social Security and was told that she was subject to the GPO/WEP. Unfortunately, I didn't get the chance to listen in on that call. Social Security call takers are knowledgeable and hardworking but they are understaffed and rushed. The agency has closed numerous field offices and cutback on personnel. If someone called up and said, "I'm going to get a government pension—am I subject to an offset?" the answer may well have been a quick YES. But in reality, she is not subject to any special formulas or rules.

Rumor #5: When I die, my teacher pension that is then paid to my husband will reduce his Social Security that he earned from his own earnings record. Definitely not true. The only person whose Social Security can be affected by a pension from outside of the SSA system is the person who earned the pension; not the spouse. This a rumor I hear a lot. It needs to be stated, more than once, that the *Windfall Elimination Provision* formula does not apply to people who receive widow or widower benefits from a pension fund for work that the spouse, when he or she was alive, worked outside of the Social Security System.

Help social security get it right. The Social Security application for benefits supports my comments on Rumor #4 and Rumor #5. Question 14(a) of the application asks:

"are you entitled to, or do you expect to be entitled to, a pension…based on **your** work **not** covered by Social Security?" (emphasis added).

45

The surviving spouse of a teacher (Rumor #5) is not going to receive a pension based on his or her *own* work not covered by Social Security. The surviving spouse is going to receive a survivor's pension based on *the decedent's* work not covered by Social Security. The answer in this case to Question 14(a) is, therefore, no. And as a result of the answer and the specific circumstances, the WEP does not apply.

And while we are examining Question 14(a), note that an employee who *does* participate in Social Security while in public service (such as our IMRF or similar pensioner in Rumor #4) is not going to receive a pension from his or her work not covered by Social Security. Their work *is* covered by Social Security. The answer to Question 14(a) is, therefore, no. And as a result of the answer and the specific circumstances, the WEP does not apply.

> **Rumor #6: A retired firefighter is getting a Social Security check of $9 per month.** Remember, this is one of the rumors that first drew my attention back in Skokie in the 1980s. It is not possible now, and was not possible back then, to receive a Social Security retirement benefit that is that low. The Social Security field representative that we met with back in 1989 didn't want to say how low of a benefit could possibly be paid, but she did laugh at the $9 rumor. I compute the lowest possible benefit under the WEP for a person who worked only enough time and low wages to get forty credits to be $52 per month today. And, of course, most public workers will qualify for higher benefits.

But, when I first blew off the $9 rumor, I didn't think about the monthly premium for Medicare Part-B. This premium is most often paid by the retiree via deduction from a Social Security check. The 2019 cost is $135; back in 1989 it was $32. The reason I finally thought of this is that a retired teacher friend gets a Social Security check of about $12 *after deduction of the Medicare B premium.*

So, was it possible that a retired Skokie firefighter had a Social Security benefit back in 1989 of $41 and, after the Medicare B premium was deducted, the net check was $9? Yes, that was possible.

I guess some firehouse rumors are better than others!

6 SOCIAL SECURITY AND PUBLIC EMPLOYEES: WRAP-UP

THERE IS A LOT OF information in the chapters you just read. Let's summarize where we have traveled:

Social Security benefits are based on a worker's wages over his or her working life, essentially 35 years. Forty credits (usually ten years) must be worked to obtain any benefit.

Many state and local employees are in Social Security for their career work; they are treated exactly like the private sector workforce.

About 28%, maybe 6.5 million people, do *not* participate in Social Security at their public service jobs. However, most will earn Social Security benefits from work before, during, and after their public careers. They will generally earn a lower benefit than their private sector counterparts because of the many higher income years that they work outside of Social Security.

Social Security benefits are progressively designed to pay higher benefits to low income wage earners. Workers who *are not* in Social Security for their career jobs are not low income workers, but the Social Security formula would at first see them as that. Because of this, the calculations of these workers' Social Security benefits are modified.

Benefits from their own Social Security earnings are calculated differently to prohibit a "windfall." If retiring today, they would receive a Social Security benefit that is 40% to 56% lower but not more than $480 lower than the benefit produced by the standard, progressive formula. A more precise estimate is available using the online Benefit Calculator, WEP Version. See the *Windfall Elimination Provision.*

Social Security Benefits from their spouse's record, both as a spouse and a widow(er) are offset, essentially eliminated, by their public pension. See the *Government Pension Offset.*

By any objective measurement, the GPO and the WEP are not unfair to the public employee workforce, although the WEP could be improved to protect against over-correction. Legislation to address this is in the pipeline.

The "three-legged stool" of retirement income includes pension, Social Security, and personal savings. For some teachers, firefighters, police officers and others, the Social Security leg will be lessened by a career outside of Social Security. Generally higher pension benefits than the private sector workforce make up for lack of Social Security coverage at the public entity. This should be remembered when public employee pensions are unjustly criticized.

IS SOCIAL SECURITY PARTICIPATION VALUABLE?

To be polite, heck yes! There is always a benefit to earning Social Security covered wages. Why even raise the question? It's because I've actually heard from government retirees who didn't want to take Social Security-covered jobs after retirement because "the formulas are all messed up" or some similar, imaginary problem. This is not true. With a subsequent employer paying half of the cost, there is no reason not to pay the 6.2% payroll deduction and earn credit towards a monthly benefit, even under the WEP formula. You can't gain the equivalent of that benefit investing on your own. If anyone thinks otherwise, ask him to show you the math.

This applies across the board. For a young professional who only has a few years in Social Security before entering non-SSA participating public service, it will pay in the long run for him or her to gain forty (40) credits/quarters and qualify. For someone who has already achieved Social Security eligibility and is retiring from teaching or police/fire/city hall, adding to their Social Security record prior to attaining age 62 or even later will improve their Social Security benefit.

Additionally, the earlier in your working life that you earn Social Security eligibility, the earlier you will attain eligibility for Social Security disability benefits. I haven't talked much about SSA disability benefits other than in the general introduction. But if a worker becomes disabled *and* the medical condition also qualifies for Social Security disability benefits, he or she may be able to collect Social Security disability benefits. Granted the SSA disability benefit will be fairly small if the career work is outside of Social Security, but that small monthly disability check could still provide a person with critical income at a time when it is sorely needed.

QUESTIONS AND ANSWERS

I'll conclude with a brief Q&A. Similar to the chapter on rumors, these are questions that I have received over the years and a review will help you improve your knowledge on these important topics.

Q. *I will earn a pension as a firefighter in a department that didn't participate in Social Security. What is the effect of that on the Social Security that I qualified for from other jobs?*

A. There are two effects on your eventual Social Security benefits that result from your pension outside of Social Security.

If you are or were married, you will generally not be able to obtain any benefit from your spouse's record. This is due to a provision called the *Government Pension Offset* or GPO. As far as your own record of Social Security wages, you will receive a monthly benefit but it will be calculated using a modified formula under the *Windfall Elimination Provision* or WEP. This is done because low wage earners from the private sector workforce are paid a disproportionately higher Social Security benefit. SSA doesn't want to pay that poor man's higher monthly benefit to you because you are not a low wage earner. The WEP accomplishes that modification in a way that results in the amount you receive from Social Security being somewhat the same wage replacement rate as other workers with whom you had similar lifetime wages.

Q. *I was told that I wouldn't get any Social Security benefit from my part-time work because of my time as a public school teacher outside of Social Security. Is that true?*

A. No, it is not true. Every worker who attains forty quarters (or "credits") in Social Security will receive a benefit regardless of their work in fire, police, teaching or other public services. Statements by anyone that you will not receive a benefit are the worst extreme of the rumors surrounding this subject.

Q. *I work in a police agency that is in Social Security. I called the Social Security 800-number and was told that my Social Security would be reduced because of my police work. Is that true?*

A. No, it is not true that your Social Security benefit would be reduced as a result of your current police employment. Social Security historically has had a great customer service capability, but it has been cut back due to budget restrictions. You most likely told the overworked call taker that "I have a government pension" or "I have a police pension" and the Social Security employee went right to the script about the GPO and WEP. But those provisions DO NOT apply to persons who were *in* Social Security during their public safety, teaching or other government careers.

Q. *Is my wife's Social Security benefit affected in any way by my work as a water plant operator who did <u>not</u> participate in Social Security during my public service career? How about when I die?*

A. Absolutely not. She is entitled to all of the SSA benefit she earned on her own. And, if you die first and she receives a survivor benefit from your public pension plan, this will not impact the Social Security benefit that she would earn from her own record of Social Security covered employment. Nothing in the GPO or WEP affects the benefit that a government worker's husband or wife will earn on their own.

Q. *I am a Chicago police officer and my wife is a Chicago school teacher. Neither of us participates in Social Security. However, we both have enough credit from work prior to city employment to qualify for Social Security. How much can we expect to receive in Social Security benefits?*

A. Not much. You are both working in careers outside of Social Security, so your actual time in Social Security is limited. And the wages that you earned when you participated in SSA were most likely fairly low compared to your professional earnings. So, you have a small amount of time in the Social Security system and did not earn a lot of money during that time.

You can estimate a benefit using the WEP formula in the preceding chapter or sign on to *ssa.gov* for a personal account and use your own information to simulate different scenarios.

I want to be cautious about coming up with any type of estimate for you, since everyone's situation is different. If you'll remember that—everyone's situation is different—I'll give an example using the earnings of a possibly typical worker who was discussed earlier in Chapter 3. That person was a hypothetical public employee who had inflation-adjusted earnings as follows: $15,000 yearly for five years, then no Social Security earnings during a public service career, then $50,000 annually for ten years.

Using today's formula's, that person's Social Security benefit at the Full Retirement Age would be $515 per month, calculated using the WEP formula. More earnings than those surmised would produce a higher benefit, lower earnings would create a lower benefit.

Q. *I work at a public agency job that is covered by Social Security. I understand that the GPO and WEP do not apply to me. But what if I retire from here and go to a job where there is not Social Security participation? Can that hurt me in any way?*

A.   This is a question I received at a seminar presentation and it was a great question. I'll answer it by talking directly to the reader of this book as opposed to replying to a hypothetical questioner.

The police officer was ready to retire from a city that participated in Social Security. But because of the historical mixing of participating and nonparticipating entities in Illinois, there was the possibility that he might have a second career at a police department that does *not* participate in Social Security. If he gets a pension from that second job, even a small one, could it affect his Social Security he earned from his first full-time police career?

The technical answer is yes, he could be affected by taking that second job that is outside of Social Security; the complete answer is almost assuredly NO.

If he receives a pension from the second job, he will have a pension from work outside of Social Security. The GPO and the WEP will turn "on." While he was previously immune from those provisions because his police work was *in* Social Security, that will no longer be the case.

But, should he be concerned about the *Government Pension Offset*? No. Even without the GPO, he is never going to receive a Social Security benefit from his wife's earnings record. He has his own full-time professional wages covered by Social Security which will produce a Social Security benefit that is far in excess of one-half of his wife's benefit, even if she is a CEO and earns the highest benefit payable. So there is simply no spousal benefit to be had here, GPO or no GPO. His second career outside of Social Security simply can't do him any harm.

And, he most likely won't care about the *Windfall Elimination Provision* (WEP) either. The impact of this provision begins to wear-away if a person has twenty-one years of substantial earnings under Social Security and it shuts off completely upon attaining thirty years of substantial earnings. As this questioner had a full first career in police work covered by Social Security, he assuredly has twenty-one years of service, closer to or exceeding thirty years. Thus, he has "substantial earnings" that greatly mitigate or completely turn off the WEP.

This police officer will likely experience no impact on his Social Security benefits if he qualifies for a small pension from a second employer that happens to be outside of Social Security. If he wants that second career, he should go for it.

ADDITIONAL RESOURCES 7

I HOPE YOU HAVE ENJOYED this review of how Social Security benefits are impacted by a state or local government pension from work outside of the Social Security system.

You can grow your knowledge of your own benefits by checking out the following resources, among others:

The *Government Pension Offset* (SSA Publication 05-10007) and the *Windfall Elimination Provision* (SSA Publication 05-10045) are appended to this book. Further, many Social Security publications available online at *socialsecurity.gov* are easy to read and very informative.

Two excellent resources for a "deep dive" into the subject are whitepapers from the Congressional Research Service: "Social Security: The Government Pension Offset (GPO)," dated January 30, 2012 and "Social Security: The Windfall Elimination Provision (WEP)," updated October 22, 2019. These are relatively short documents but are packed with good detail and summary information.

Another whitepaper, "The Windfall Elimination Provision—It's Time to Correct the Math," from the Social Security Advisory Board (*ssab. gov*) discusses the possible improvements to the WEP formula to ensure that the replacement rate is virtually identical for both SSA covered and non-covered workers. This theory is the basis for the legislation recently proposed and discussed in this book. Moreover, the paper is an excellent resource for understanding the WEP, including its history.

Anything online from writer Thomas Margenau on the subject of public employees and Social Security will be worthwhile.

You can further examine the issue of why and how some public employees do not participate in Social Security by checking out the website of the National Conference of State Social Security Administrators (*ncsssa.org*). As already noted, this site will also identify your state's liaison to the Social Security Administration for public employer matters.

For a general overview of Social Security benefits, there are a lot of books out there. Two I recommend are *Social Security Made Simple* by Mike Piper and *Social Security Basics* by Devon Carroll. Both are focused on getting the reader key information as opposed to being a comprehensive resource on Social Security. Mr. Carroll's is a little longer, with more information and he maintains a website at *socialsecurityintelligence.com*. Note that he has also written a book on the WEP and GPO entitled *The Hero's Penalty: How Social Security Works for Educators*.

NOTE:
INFORMATION APPEARING ELSEWHERE

Much of this information was published earlier in the author's paperback book, *Retirement Income for Illinois Fire and Police: Pensions, Social Security and Deferred Compensation* and further appears at the website of the Illinois Public Pension Fund Association (IPPFA.org). For this book, the information has been updated to include Social Security formulas for the current year and additional information has been added that was not included in the original text.

APPENDIX 1:
WINDFALL ELIMINATION PROVISION

2019

Windfall Elimination Provision

Your Social Security retirement or disability benefits can be reduced

The Windfall Elimination Provision can affect how we calculate your retirement or disability benefit. If you work for an employer who doesn't withhold Social Security taxes from your salary, such as a government agency or an employer in another country, any retirement or disability pension you get from that work can reduce your Social Security benefits.

When your benefits can be affected

This provision can affect you when you earn a retirement or disability pension from an employer who didn't withhold Social Security taxes **and** you qualify for Social Security retirement or disability benefits from work in other jobs for which you did pay taxes.

The Windfall Elimination Provision can apply if:

- You reached 62 after 1985; or
- You became disabled after 1985; and
- You first became eligible for a monthly pension based on work where you didn't pay Social Security taxes after 1985. This rule applies even if you're still working.

This provision also affects Social Security benefits for people who performed federal service under the Civil Service Retirement System (CSRS) after 1956. We won't reduce your Social Security benefit amounts if you only performed federal service under a system such as the Federal Employees' Retirement System (FERS). Social Security taxes are withheld for workers under FERS.

How it works

Social Security benefits are intended to replace only some of a worker's pre-retirement earnings.

We base your Social Security benefit on your average monthly earnings adjusted for average wage growth. We separate your average earnings into three amounts and multiply the amounts using three factors to compute your full Primary Insurance Amount (PIA). For example, for a worker who turns 62 in 2019, the first $926 of average monthly earnings is multiplied by 90 percent; earnings between $926 and $5,583 by 32 percent; and the balance by 15 percent. The sum of the three amounts equals the PIA which is then decreased or increased depending on whether the worker starts benefits before or after full retirement age (FRA). This formula produces the monthly payment amount.

When we apply this formula, the percentage of career average earnings paid to lower-paid workers is greater than higher-paid workers. For example, workers age 62 in 2019, with average earnings of $3,000 per month could receive a benefit at FRA of $1,497 (approximately 49 percent) of their pre-retirement earnings increased by applicable cost of living adjustments (COLAs). For a worker with average earnings of $8,000 per month, the benefit starting at FRA could be $2,686 (approximately 33 percent) plus COLAs. However, if either of these workers start benefits earlier, we'll reduce their monthly benefit.

Why we use a different formula

Before 1983, people whose primary job wasn't covered by Social Security had their Social Security benefits calculated as if they were long-term, low-wage workers. They had the advantage of receiving a Social Security benefit representing a higher percentage of their earnings, plus a pension from a job for which they didn't pay Social Security taxes. Congress passed the Windfall Elimination Provision to remove that advantage.

Under the provision, we reduce the 90 percent factor in our formula and phase it in for workers who reached age 62 or became disabled between 1986 and 1989. For people who reach 62 or became disabled in 1990 or later, we reduce the 90 percent factor to as little as 40 percent.

Some exceptions

The Windfall Elimination Provision doesn't apply if:

- You're a federal worker first hired after December 31, 1983;
- You're an employee of a non-profit organization who was first hired after December 31, 1983;
- Your only pension is for railroad employment;
- The only work you performed for which you didn't pay Social Security taxes was before 1957; or
- You have 30 or more years of substantial earnings under Social Security.

The Windfall Elimination Provision doesn't apply to survivors benefits. We may reduce spouses, widows, or widowers benefits because of another law. For more information, read *Government Pension Offset* (Publication No. 05-10007).

Social Security years of substantial earnings

If you have 30 or more years of substantial earnings, we don't reduce the standard 90 percent factor in our formula. See the first table that lists substantial earnings for each year.

The second table shows the percentage used to reduce the 90 percent factor depending on the number of years of substantial earnings. If you have 21 to 29 years of substantial earnings, we reduce the 90 percent factor to between 45 and 85 percent. To see the maximum amount we could reduce your benefit, visit *www.socialsecurity.gov/planners/retire/wep-chart.html*.

A guarantee

The law protects you if you get a low pension. We won't reduce your Social Security benefit by more than half of your pension for earnings after 1956 on which you didn't pay Social Security taxes.

Contacting Social Security

The most convenient way to contact us anytime, anywhere is to visit *www.socialsecurity.gov*. There, you can: apply for benefits; open a *my Social Security* account, which you can use to review your *Social Security Statement*, verify your earnings, print a benefit verification letter, change your direct deposit information, request a replacement Medicare card, and get a replacement SSA-1099/1042S; obtain valuable information; find publications; get answers to frequently asked questions; and much more.

If you don't have access to the internet, we offer many automated services by telephone, 24 hours a day, 7 days a week. Call us toll-free at **1-800-772-1213** or at our TTY number, **1-800-325-0778**, if you're deaf or hard of hearing.

If you need to speak to a person, we can answer your calls from 7 a.m. to 7 p.m., Monday through Friday. We ask for your patience during busy periods since you may experience a higher than usual rate of busy signals and longer hold times to speak to us. We look forward to serving you.

Year	Substantial earnings	Year	Substantial earnings
1937–1954	$900	1992	$10,350
1955–1958	$1,050	1993	$10,725
1959–1965	$1,200	1994	$11,250
1966–1967	$1,650	1995	$11,325
1968–1971	$1,950	1996	$11,625
1972	$2,250	1997	$12,150
1973	$2,700	1998	$12,675
1974	$3,300	1999	$13,425
1975	$3,525	2000	$14,175
1976	$3,825	2001	$14,925
1977	$4,125	2002	$15,750
1978	$4,425	2003	$16,125
1979	$4,725	2004	$16,275
1980	$5,100	2005	$16,725
1981	$5,550	2006	$17,475
1982	$6,075	2007	$18,150
1983	$6,675	2008	$18,975
1984	$7,050	2009–2011	$19,800
1985	$7,425	2012	$20,475
1986	$7,875	2013	$21,075
1987	$8,175	2014	$21,750
1988	$8,400	2015-2016	$22,050
1989	$8,925	2017	$23,625
1990	$9,525	2018	$23,850
1991	$9,900	2019	$24,675

Years of substantial earnings	Percentage
30 or more	90 percent
29	85 percent
28	80 percent
27	75 percent
26	70 percent
25	65 percent
24	60 percent
23	55 percent
22	50 percent
21	45 percent
20 or less	40 percent

Securing today and tomorrow

Social Security Administration
Publication No. 05-10045 | ICN 460275 | Unit of Issue — HD (one hundred)
January 2019 (Recycle prior editions)
Windfall Elimination Provision
Produced and published at U.S. taxpayer expense

△ Printed on recycled paper

APPENDIX 2:
GOVERNMENT PENSION OFFSET

 Government Pension Offset

A law that affects spouses and widows or widowers

If you receive a retirement or disability pension from a federal, state, or local government based on your own work for which you didn't pay Social Security taxes, we may reduce your Social Security spouses or widows or widowers benefits. This fact sheet provides answers to questions you may have about the reduction.

How much will my Social Security benefits be reduced?

We'll reduce your Social Security benefits by two-thirds of your government pension. In other words, if you get a monthly civil service pension of $600, two-thirds of that, or $400, must be deducted from your Social Security benefits. For example, if you're eligible for a $500 spouses, widows, or widowers benefit from Social Security, you'll get $100 a month from Social Security ($500 − $400 = $100). If two-thirds of your government pension is more than your Social Security benefit, your benefit could be reduced to zero.

If you take your government pension annuity in a lump sum, Social Security will calculate the reduction as if you chose to get monthly benefit payments from your government work.

Why will my Social Security benefits be reduced?

Benefits we pay to spouses, widows, and widowers are "dependent" benefits. Set up in the 1930s, these benefits were to compensate spouses who stayed home to raise a family and were financially dependent on the working spouse. It's now common for both spouses to work, each earning their own Social Security retirement benefit. The law requires a person's spouse, widow, or widower benefit to be offset by the dollar amount of their own retirement benefit.

For example, if a woman worked and earned her own $800 monthly Social Security benefit, but was also due a $500 spouse's benefit on her husband's record, we couldn't pay that spouse's benefit because her own benefit offsets it. Before enactment of the Government Pension Offset law, if that same woman was a government employee who didn't pay into Social Security and earned an $800 government pension, there was no offset. We had to pay her a full spouse's benefit and her full government pension.

If this person's government work had been subject to Social Security taxes, we would reduce any spouse, widow, or widower benefit because of their own Social Security retirement benefit. The Government Pension Offset ensures that we calculate the benefits of government employees who don't pay Social Security taxes the same as workers in the private sector who pay Social Security taxes.

When won't my Social Security benefits be reduced?

Generally, we won't reduce your Social Security benefits as a spouse, widow, or widower if you:

- Receive a government pension that's not based on your earnings; or
- Are a federal (including Civil Service Offset), state, or local government employee and your government pension is from a job for which you paid Social Security taxes; and:
  —Your last day of employment (that your pension is based on) is before July 1, 2004; or
  —You filed for and were entitled to spouses, widows, or widowers benefits before April 1, 2004 (you may work your last day in Social Security covered employment at any time); or
  —You paid Social Security taxes on your earnings during the last 60 months of government service. (Under certain

(over)

63

APPENDIX 2 (PAGE 2):
GOVERNMENT PENSION OFFSET

conditions, we require fewer than 60 months for people whose last day of employment falls after June 30, 2004, and before March 2, 2009.)

There are other situations for which we won't reduce your Social Security benefits as a spouse, widow, or widower; for example, if you:

- Are a federal employee who switched from the Civil Service Retirement System (CSRS) to the Federal Employees' Retirement System (FERS) after December 31, 1987; and:

  —Your last day of service (that your pension is based on) is before July 1, 2004;

  —You paid Social Security taxes on your earnings for 60 months or more during the period beginning January 1988 and ending with the first month of entitlement to benefits; or

  —You filed for and were entitled to spouses, widows, or widowers benefits before April 1, 2004 (you may work your last day in Social Security covered employment at any time).

- Received, or were eligible to receive, a government pension before December 1982 and meet all the requirements for Social Security spouse's benefits in effect in January 1977; or

- Received, or were eligible to receive, a federal, state, or local government pension before July 1, 1983, and were receiving one-half support from your spouse.

Note: A Civil Service Offset employee is a federal employee, rehired after December 31, 1983, following a break in service of more than 365 days, with five years of prior CSRS coverage.

What about Medicare?

Even if you don't get benefit payments from your spouse's work, you can still get Medicare at age 65 on your spouse's record if you aren't eligible for it on your own record.

Can I still get Social Security benefits from my own work?

The offset applies only to Social Security benefits as a spouse, or widow, or widower. However, we may reduce your own benefits because of another provision. For more information, go online to read *Windfall Elimination Provision* (Publication No. 05-10045).

Contacting Social Security

The most convenient way to contact us anytime, anywhere is to visit ***www.socialsecurity.gov***. There, you can: apply for benefits; open a *my* Social Security account, which you can use to review your *Social Security Statement*, verify your earnings, print a benefit verification letter, change your direct deposit information, request a replacement Medicare card, and get a replacement SSA-1099/1042S; obtain valuable information; find publications; get answers to frequently asked questions; and much more.

If you don't have access to the internet, we offer many automated services by telephone, 24 hours a day, 7 days a week. Call us toll-free at **1-800-772-1213** or at our TTY number, **1-800-325-0778**, if you're deaf or hard of hearing.

If you need to speak to a person, we can answer your calls from 7 a.m. to 7 p.m., Monday through Friday. We ask for your patience during busy periods since you may experience higher than usual rate of busy signals and longer hold times to speak to us. We look forward to serving you.

Securing today and tomorrow

Social Security Administration
Publication No. 05-10007 | ICN 451453 | Unit of Issue — HD (one hundred)
May 2019 (Recycle prior editions)
Government Pension Offset
Produced and published at U.S. taxpayer expense

ACKNOWLEDGMENTS

Thanks to some people who assisted me in this undertaking~

First and foremost, the academics and professionals who have researched
and communicated Social Security issues before I undertook this effort
should be acknowledged. See the references section at the end of this book
and consider expanding your knowledge by taking advantage of theirs.

The Board of the Illinois Public Pension Fund Association (IPPFA) supported
this project, especially President Jim McNamee and his contribution of the
Foreword. Office assistant Mandy Paciorkowski helped with printing
and copying and took many a late-night email from me at home and had
the work product ready for review when I arrived at the office.

And old friend and public pension guru, Stan Helgerson, reviewed
the draft and provided valuable direction.

My wife Kathy and her sister Karen Binkerd, both affected teacher retirees,
reviewed the draft from that special perspective.

My daughter, Suzanne Ryan Jackson, provided a final,
professional look through.

This institutional and personal support is greatly appreciated,
but it should be reiterated that while I do not anticipate that I made any
mistakes, any errors in content or description are my responsibility alone.

And thanks to the many friends and relatives whose first names
happen to pop up in the examples used to illuminate the subject.

REFERENCES

GOVERNMENT REPORTS

Meyerson, Noah. "How Social Security Benefits Are Computed: In Brief." *Congressional Research Service.* (May 12, 2014).

Shelton, Alison M. *Social Security: The Government Pension Offset.* Washington: Library of Congress, Congressional Research Service. January 30, 2012. Updated June 12, 2019 by author Zhe Li.

Li, Zhe, *Social Security: The Windfall Elimination Provision.* Washington: Library of Congress, Congressional Research Service. Updated October 22, 2019.

NEWSPAPERS

Ruffenach, Glenn. "What You Don't Know about Social Security—but Should." *Wall Street Journal.* (June 22, 2014).

Miller, Mark. "7 of Your Most Burning Questions on Social Security (with Answers)," *New York Times.* (August 2, 2019).

PRESENTATIONS

Brown, Alex (National Association of State Retirement Administrators), "Public Pension Landscape and Trends," *Presentation to the Illinois Public Pension Fund Association Roundtable.* Chicago, IL. (July 29 2019).

Weber, A.J. "Social Security Explanation," *Presentation to the Illinois Professional Firefighters Association Spring Seminar.* Addison IL. (May 1, 2015).

BOOKS

Carroll, Devin, *Social Security Basics: 9 Essentials that Everyone Should Know.* Amazon.com.

Carroll, Devin, *The Hero's Penalty: How Social Security Works for Educators.* Amazon.com.

Munnell, Alicia, *State and Local Pensions: What Now?* Brookings Institution Press. 2012.

Piper, Mike, *Social Security Made Simple,* Simple Subjects LLC, 2019.

OTHER

Social Security Advisory Board, "The Windfall Elimination Provision—It's Time to Correct the Math," *sssb.gov.* (October 1, 2015).

Caplinger, Dan, "Why Does Social Security Leave Out Teachers in These 15 States," Motelyfool.com. (October 7, 2018).

Turner, Cory, "Why More than a Million Teachers Can't Use Social Security," *Npr.org.* (April 20, 2018).

National Association of State Retirement Administrators, "Social Security Coverage." *Nasra.org.*

Kan, Leslie and Aldeman, Chad, "Uncovered: Social Security, Retirement Uncertainty and 1 Million Teachers," *TeacherPensions.org,* 2014.

Aldeman, Chad and Rotherham, Andrew, "Friends without Benefits: How states systematically shortchange teachers' retirement and threaten their retirement security," *TeacherPensions.org.* 2014.

Made in the USA
Columbia, SC
30 April 2020